Original title:
The Answer to Life: Still Pending

Copyright © 2025 Creative Arts Management OÜ
All rights reserved.

Author: Giselle Montgomery
ISBN HARDBACK: 978-1-80566-137-5
ISBN PAPERBACK: 978-1-80566-432-1

Compromises With Certainty

In search of wisdom, I took a peek,
Stumbled on questions that made me weak.
Pondering choices with socks in a twist,
I chuckled aloud—was that on the list?

I tried to decipher the meaning of cheese,
Met a wise cat who just wanted some peas.
He winked and he said, 'Just follow the crumbs,
For life's a big joke, and we're all just clowns.'

With coffee in hand, I danced with a spoon,
Debating the universe under a moon.
"Does it matter," I asked, "if my toast's not right?"
The bread just smiled, "You'll be fine, take a bite!"

A rubber chicken joined in with a quack,
Claiming the secrets were hidden in a snack.
As laughter erupted from each little thing,
I found my conclusion in a bowl of string.

So here's to the puzzles and playful delight,
In a world where confusion dances at night.
We may never find answers, but hey, that's okay,
Let's savor the questions that brighten our day!

Questions Beneath the Surface

Why do cows wear bells so bright?
They answer questions in the night.
Do we know if fish can sing?
Or why squirrels run from everything?

Is it true that birds can't swim?
And does a cat think it's a whim?
Each question bounces through my head,
Like pillows soft, where dreams are fed.

Threads of Uncertainty Spun

What if pancakes could wear hats?
Would they chat with playful cats?
Sticky syrup debates with toast,
Who'd win the breakfast party most?

Bananas think they're in a race,
But oranges always win the chase.
And grapes just giggle when we talk,
As jellybeans do their silly walk.

Chronicles of the Unwritten

Once a turtle decided to run,
He slid on ice, thought it was fun.
A snail challenged him to a chase,
But got stuck in the same old place.

A time-traveling beetle cried,
For he just couldn't find his ride.
Pages unwritten, tales on pause,
Wondering what the world applause.

Journeys Through the Undiscovered

Let's journey where no one has been,
To places odd where fish wear skin.
The caves of cheese and hills of cake,
  Where rules of logic take a break.

On roads made of jelly, we shall roam,
In a land where every word feels like home.
Exploring nonsense, laughter we'll find,
  The treasure chest of a silly mind.

The Thrum of Anticipation

A cat in a hat, so snug and so nice,
Waiting for wisdom, as if it's a slice.
Tick-tock goes the clock, it hints and it teases,
While life plays its games, and we're just the pieces.

Balloons float by, all filled with delight,
Each one a question, all taking flight.
We chase after answers, with snacks and some cheer,
As life keeps on spinning, the fun's always near.

Bridges to the Undefined

I built a grand bridge, but it leads to a wall,
A sign says 'Proceed,' but I trip and I fall.
An avocado toast plays a song in my head,
While I ponder the meaning—still not out of bed.

The squirrels have a meeting, they all take a vote,
Should we jump to conclusions or just stay afloat?
As I sip my tea, the universe grins,
And whispers sweet nothings, as chaos begins.

Resounding Silences

In the echo of silence, there's laughter and fun,
Where whispers of wisdom are spun by the sun.
A banana slips by, with a wink and a nod,
As I search for the secret, feeling a bit odd.

A fish in a sweater swims laps by the door,
What does it mean? Who could ask for more?
The jokes write themselves as the void holds its breath,
In the quietest chuckles, there's life and there's death.

Echoes of Tomorrow

Tomorrow is coming, it's just running late,
With a grin and a dance, oh, what a fate!
I knock on its door, but it shimmies away,
As I chase down the moments like children at play.

Clouds shaped like questions float high in the sky,
They giggle and tumble, each one a sly lie.
A marshmallow world where the laughter's the guide,
Whispers of answers make giggles collide.

The Longing for Clarity

In a world of questions, we stumble and sway,
Searching for answers, yet lost in the play.
Why did the chicken cross over the street?
To find a good punchline, or something to eat?

We ride on the merry-go-round of our dreams,
Chasing bright rainbows and pie-in-the-sky schemes.
With logic so wobbly, we laugh and we pout,
Is anyone certain? I seriously doubt!

Spaces Between the Notes

In the music of life, we dance out of tune,
Trying to hum harmony under a bright moon.
What if the silence is making the sound?
A riddle wrapped tightly, where answers are drowned?

We spin like a record that's stuck on repeat,
Stumbling through verses, oh, isn't it sweet?
With each little hiccup, we chuckle and cheer,
Perhaps the best questions are ones we hold dear!

The Canvas Unframed

With splatters of color, we paint on the wall,
Searching for meaning in strips of pale shawl.
What's with the splashes? It's all just absurd!
A masterpiece waiting—a picture unheard!

Yet here we are, drawing the lines ever thin,
Asking the universe where do we begin?
The art that we chase is just whimsically wild,
What's life without laughter? Let's stay like a child!

Portals to Possibility

Through doors made of dreams, we skip and we hop,
Finding the humor in every time we flop.
If life's a big circus, where's all of the fun?
Where's the great punchline? Oh, I'm not the one!

With each little mishap, we giggle and sway,
Turning blunders to gold in the light of the day.
The mystery thickens, like cream in a stew,
To find laughter's key unlocks wonders anew!

Shadows of What Could Be

In the shadows, we search for glee,
Where laughter dances, wild and free.
Questions linger in the air,
Like socks lost in a laundry dare.

Frustration wraps like a cozy quilt,
As bright ideas are slowly built.
Each whimsy thought takes a wild flight,
While we chase giggles into the night.

Yet dreams parade with glorious flair,
A carnival ride we all must share.
In jest we find a glimmering cue,
That something grand may just come through.

Oh, shadows tease with a cheeky grin,
While we sip coffee, thick as sin.
We laugh aloud at our silly plight,
In search of meaning, maybe tonight.

Labors of Love and Doubt

With love, we toil amidst the jest,
Digging for sense in a playful quest.
Doubt wears a hat, oh fancy and bright,
As we juggle reason and sheer delight.

Crafting our dreams with glitter and glue,
Plans spiral out like a crazy zoo.
Each effort crowned with a chuckle loud,
As we dance through the chaos, lost but proud.

A labor of love, messy as pie,
Full of blunders that make us sigh.
Yet in each mistake, a lesson learned,
That humor's the lamp for which we yearn.

So here we stand with hearts on our sleeves,
Weaving tales where laughter believes.
In this wild dance of whimsy and doubt,
The best things bloom, without a route.

The Quest for Light Beyond the Veil

Behind the veil, we peek with care,
Hoping to find some wisdom rare.
Instead, we're met with a playful tease,
Like a cat chasing its own noisy sneeze.

Finding light is like herding cats,
With cosmic giggles and curious spats.
We navigate the mystery, lively and bold,
In this treasure hunt, both hot and cold.

Each flicker shines with absurd delight,
Illuminating paths with wit and fright.
The search continues, a merry charade,
With each wisecrack, clarity fades.

But we march on, with spirits spry,
Loving the dance under the cosmic sky.
In the laughter, we find our trail,
Though the light ahead remains a tale.

Fleeting Moments of Understanding

A flash of insight, quick as a wink,
Moments that dash before we think.
Like bubbles of wisdom that rise and pop,
Leaving us giggling, then ready to stop.

In conversations held 'round the block,
Ideas bounce like a rubbery rock.
We grasp at thoughts, then let them slide,
In this hilarious, chaotic ride.

With each revelation, a silly cheer,
As understanding dashes, yet reappears.
We scribble notes on napkins wide,
If only wisdom could take us for a ride.

So we embrace these glimmers of fun,
With laughter echoing, never done.
In fleeting moments, we find our way,
With chuckles and musings for another day.

Chronicles of the Unanswered

In a land of questions wide,
With answers stuck in a slide,
The sheep debate in a flock,
While the clock just ticks and tocks.

Philosophers sip their tea,
Pondering what may be free,
The biscuit crumbs in their head,
Are tangled thoughts left for dead.

Cats nap as we scratch our chins,
While life spins on a twin fins,
The fridge hums a perfect tune,
Yet we dance to an empty room.

So let's laugh while we can try,
To question the stars in the sky,
For in absurdity, we might find,
The truth is just a state of mind.

Tides of Speculation

Waves of thoughts crash on the shore,
Do we really know what's in store?
Seagulls squawk about the fate,
While our minds just seem to skate.

Do fish ponder with their gills?
About human dreams and thrills?
Underwater parties in the sea,
Where logic swims wild and free.

Scientists flash their calculators,
They debate like animated narrators,
Numbers dance, jump, and swirl,
While we just toss and twirl.

Let's raise a glass to the absurd,
For it's the craziest thoughts that stirred,
In this tide where we must wait,
Laughter is our best debate.

Dimensions of Thought

In the cube of intellect's room,
Ideas bloom and sometimes fume,
Each thought a quirky little sprite,
That twirls around and takes flight.

We measure depth in a straight line,
But circles wiggle and entwine,
What's up may just be down,
In this circus, we all clown.

Multi-dimensions dance and play,
In every odd and silly way,
As paradox wears a funny hat,
Curiosity purrs like a cat.

So join the jesters of the mind,
In this playground we will find,
That logic can trip on a stair,
And laughter's everywhere!

Horizons of Inquiry

Look past the horizon we chase,
With questions that quicken the pace,
Beyond the edge of what we see,
Lies a land of curiosity.

Why do birds sing, who knows?
Perhaps they're the poets in rows,
While trees shake their leafy heads,
Whispering secrets in their beds.

We map the stars and wonder why,
As comets zoom and planets sigh,
The universe plays hide and seek,
With answers that feel quite bleak.

So let's toast to the great unknown,
With every thought that's ever grown,
In this vast and silly quest,
The joy of inquiry is the best!

Hints of Existence

In the fridge, a snack awaits,
Is that my purpose? Who dictates?
Lost my keys, can't find the way,
Is pondering life just a delay?

Cats know more than they let on,
Whiskers twitching with a yawn.
Should I chase my dreams or nap?
Got my doubts, let's set a trap.

Philosophers sip their tea,
Do they ponder as I flee?
Every answer feels like a tease,
Maybe life's just meant to fleece.

Here I sit, among the grind,
With giggles echoing in my mind.
Existence is just a quirky jest,
Can I sign up for a curious quest?

The Riddle of Being

Do I exist, or is this fake?
In my cereal, I spy a flake.
Ask a taco, ask a shoe,
Where's the logic? No clue too.

Pondering life like it's a puzzle,
Found my shoe in yesterday's muzzle.
Did I lose my way or my rhyme?
Each tick-tock feels like a crime.

Why does laughter hold such weight?
In the park, I contemplate.
A squirrel shimmies, then it sprints,
Should I join in? Life's little hints.

Philosophy's a game for fun,
Beneath the sun, I just want to run.
Yet here I sit, so perplexed,
What's next in this wild text?

Journeys Yet to Conclude

Walking paths with socks mismatched,
Is this fashion? I'm detached.
The map is lost, GPS confused,
This journey's fun, yet I feel used.

Chasing dreams like a rubber ball,
Running from answers that seem so small.
Each turn I take, a random dance,
Is this just fate, or happenstance?

Bumps on roads, they make me laugh,
On this trip, I grab a graph.
Every twist feels like a joke,
Am I the punchline? Life bespoke.

But oh, the tales I could relay,
If I could find a clearer way.
Through laughter missteps, I will roam,
At least I've got my goofy home.

Threads of Curiosity

Here I weave, what's this delight?
Threads of questions, day and night.
Where do socks go when they hide?
Is there a land where lost things bide?

Tickled by thoughts of grand design,
Do trees giggle when they entwine?
What's beneath that talking toad?
Does it know life's winding road?

Bubbles pop with perplexing flair,
Who invented this wild affair?
Twirling ideas, I spin around,
In laughter's echoes, wisdom's found.

So here I sit, with tangled thought,
Curious threads, oh what a lot!
Each question leads, yet leaves me spun,
In this silly game, I'll have my fun.

Existence's Elusive Riddle

Life's a puzzle, missing pieces,
Searching for meaning, it never ceases.
Cats are plotting with the mice,
Together they roll the dice.

Coffee spills on thoughts of grand,
Socks are mismatched, isn't it bland?
Clocks tick loud, yet time stands still,
We chase our tails, against our will.

Aliens might just be on break,
While we're all here, for goodness' sake.
Life's just a sitcom, without a cue,
Starring me, and definitely you.

And when the sun sets and stars ignite,
We all ponder this cosmic byte.
But the punchline's lost in the air,
Finders keepers, but who knows where?

Searching for Clarity in the Fog

Through the haze, we squint and glance,
Hoping for insight, a second chance.
But all we find are shoes unpaired,
And thoughts that seem forever ensnared.

In a world of soup-like lacks,
We wander off the beaten tracks.
Fridges filled with leftovers past,
Wonder if time flies too fast.

The wisdom sought from coffee grinds,
Might just be jumbled, like our minds.
As clouds of doubt arise and swell,
We laugh and wonder; all is well.

Underneath this grayish dome,
We seek a sign to lead us home.
But clarity's just a joke to tease,
Like trying to tickle a sneezing sneeze.

Echoes of Unresolved Truths

In the realm of whispers low,
Truths linger like an awkward show.
A sigh escapes in search of rhyme,
While snack breaks steal the precious time.

Grandma's secrets we crave to know,
Turn out to be just stale nachos.
Ghosts are laughing as we trip,
In pursuit of sense, we often slip.

Under the bed, dust bunnies thrive,
As we ponder how to survive.
Searching for meaning in cookie dough,
It's the crumbles that steal the show.

When the universe isn't behaving,
We question if it's even saving.
So raise a toast to half-baked clues,
In the dining hall of yesterday's dues.

Whispers from the Unseen

In shadows cast by stretch and yawn,
Secrets linger, barely drawn.
The toaster hums a quiet tune,
As we dance beneath the moon.

Missing socks conspire to jest,
As we wonder if they're blessed.
Ghostly giggles flicker near,
Are they friends or just our fear?

Stirring soup, what lies beneath?
A spoonful of doubt, a pinch of grief.
Light at the end seems dim and bleak,
But laughter's the language we all seek.

So collect your dreams, your hopes, your fears,
Tell them stories, share the cheers.
For in the whispers, we find the jest,
Life's tricky game is truly the best.

Fragments of Understanding

In a sunflower's gaze, I ponder,
Does it ever feel too much?
I asked a wise old turtle,
He just gave me a gentle touch.

Cracking jokes with an owl at night,
He hoots about the stars so bright,
"Why don't they ever share a snack?"
"Too busy just keeping track!"

A squirrel scurries, nuts in mouth,
Chasing thoughts of north and south.
"Where's my acorn?" he squeaks with glee,
As if the world's made just for he.

And in my heart, a question swells,
Are we here just to trip on shells?
I chuckle with my plucky friends,
Maybe life starts where confusion ends.

Pages Yet to Be Written

In the book of life, some pages torn,
Pencils break, and ideas are born.
Chapters begin with a giggle and cheer,
But the plot twists make things unclear.

Sticky notes flutter like butterflies,
With reminders that bring out the sighs.
Doodles dance in the margins so wide,
Wishing the answers would jump in with pride.

A lion writes poetry near a stream,
Roaring verses that feel like a dream.
"Why did the chicken cross that road?"
Laughter erupts, wisdom's abode!

Yet blank lines tease like shadows in light,
What tales shall unfold under the moon's bright?
Each scribble a beacon, leading us on,
To a tale of tomorrow, forever undrawn.

Dialogues with Doubt

A cat sits pondering life's design,
"Do I chase the mouse or the sun to find?"
With a twitch of a whisker, he muses aloud,
"Perhaps I should bask where it's warm and proud!"

An ant scurries, lost in a trance,
Wondering if destiny's just a dance.
"Is the food for the feast or the drama it brings?"
In a world full of crumbs, are we queens or kings?

A dog shakes his tail, wagging with cheer,
Grins and asks, "Is life really clear?"
"Fetch me that stick, and let's make a deal,
If I throw it away, will it then be real?"

So here we sit, with giggles and sighs,
Confessions cloaked in bewildered guise.
In the chaos of chuckles, wisdom we glean,
In shadows of doubts, we sip from the sheen.

The Unsung Queries

Why do socks vanish when the dryer spins?
Is the universe laughing at our silly sins?
I ponder these questions while sipping my tea,
Contemplating life in the wildest spree.

A potato once asked, "Am I a vegetable?"
"How do I fit into this world so edible?"
With a wink of a green bean and a wink from the corn,
They laughed about dishes that might leave them worn.

A fish thinks aloud in an aquatic ballet,
"Do you think flippers were meant for the bay?"
As bubbles escape, we giggle with glee,
In a world without answers, there's so much to see.

So let's dance with our mysteries, twirl all around,
In the garden of queries, silly joys abound.
With every laugh shared, we savor the quest,
In the softness of questions, we truly are blessed.

Dancing on the Edge of Wonder

Twinkle toes on thoughts so bright,
Juggling dreams in broad daylight.
Wobbling on the brink of sense,
Smiling at the perplexing immense.

Headstands on the whims of fate,
Contorted glee at life's odd gait.
Chasing tails of curious clouds,
Laughing loud, oh what a crowd!

Twirling shards of sparkling bliss,
Every question, a playful kiss.
Ballroom dance of sweet chaos,
In this waltz, we're nunca lost.

Tiptoe past the serious wall,
From balloon men, we never fall.
With confetti made of ponder,
Who's to say what's right to wonder?

Ruminations of an Unsung Journey

Oh, the paths that lead astray,
With every turn, I see the play.
Bouncing on untraveled roads,
Giggling at my heavy loads.

I packed my bags with doubt and cheer,
Tossed in some socks, oh dear, oh dear!
Maps that twist like pretzel rods,
Who knew journeying was so odd?

Singular thoughts that cluster here,
Step right up, let's shift a gear!
Every stumble, a playful tease,
Finding joy in the next upheaves.

Humdrum thoughts now must retreat,
As I dance to a quirky beat.
Amidst the musings, I stand tall,
For every misstep, I have a ball!

In Pursuit of the Unknowable

Chasing mysteries, where'd they go?
Like socks that vanish in the flow.
Trying to catch the wind in jars,
While pondering life's own absurd bars.

With a net made of giggles and sighs,
I hunt for truths in butterfly skies.
Questions pop like fizzy drinks,
Leading me to whimsical brinks.

Where's the wisdom, I ask with flair,
As I twirl round in sparkly air?
Twirling in circles, I'm on a spree,
Finding joy in the mystery.

So let's embark on this bubbly ride,
With laughter as my trusty guide.
In the chase, I find my fun,
In unknowables, we've just begun!

The Weight of Unasked Questions

Heavy hangs the thought of doubt,
Lifting weights with mind's workout.
Questions bob like rubber ducks,
Floating past in bad luck plucks.

What if cats were dogs instead?
And penguins waddled, wildly bred?
Inquiring minds stuck in a loop,
Juggling logic inside the soup.

Pondering where socks disappear,
Flipping coins to decide what's dear.
With each toss, a wild embrace,
In the chaos, I find my place.

Unasked queries in a parade,
Marching forth in a silly charade.
With whimsy wrapped around the quest,
The weight is light, I jest my best!

Dreaming of Resolutions

I made a list of all my goals,
To reach them all, I've got my rolls.
But every time I try to start,
I end up napping—oh, the smart!

Conquer the world, that's the plan,
But first, I need to find my tan.
The couch is calling, what a tease,
Maybe tomorrow, if you please.

I dream of riches, fame, and fun,
While eating snacks, all one by one.
My resolutions, they take flight,
Just not tonight—too much bite!

So here I sit, with a grin so wide,
Planning my greatness, with snack by side.
I'll nap a bit, then start anew,
Tomorrow's bright, but today's a stew!

Labyrinths of Thought

In my mind, a maze does twist,
Thoughts go in, but don't insist.
I chase the rabbit, round and round,
But lose my way in thoughts profound.

Should I take a left or a right?
The cheese is gone, oh what a plight!
Each corner brings another task,
A simple query, too much to ask.

The exit sign just giggles loud,
"Figure it out!" it screams and crowds.
With every turn, I laugh and sigh,
Sometimes I think I'll never fly.

At last, I find a door ajar,
But it's just a cat, not a car.
I pet it softly—oh, what a plot!
In this maze of thought, I forgot what I sought!

Flickers of Insight

A light bulb flickers in my head,
But often leaves me filled with dread.
Was that a thought? Oh wait, it's gone,
Like socks that vanish—poof! And on.

I ponder life in snappy tweets,
Why can't I grasp these wily feats?
My coffee's cold, my mind's a mess,
Maybe I should just confess.

Each spark of genius, short and sweet,
But then I trip over my own feet.
I dance with thoughts that come and go,
And hope I'll catch one—maybe, who knows?

In this wild game of chase and catch,
I find new ways my thoughts can hatch.
A flicker here, a giggle there,
And life's absurdities fill the air!

The Spectrum of Wonder

With colors bright, my thoughts explode,
In puzzlement, I roam the road.
What if the sky is just a sheet?
A very grand and tasty treat!

The questions whirl like candy canes,
I ponder joy and ponder pains.
If life's a joke, I'm missing the punch,
While munching chips, I plan my lunch.

The spectrum shifts, oh what a sight,
From serious blues to playful light.
Each baffling hue brings laughter's call,
What's the point? I can't recall!

Yet as I laugh, I start to see,
That wonder thrives when we're just free.
In shades of giggles, dreams untold,
The best part's simply being bold!

Embracing the Incomplete Quest

With maps askew and crumbs of bread,
We search for truths that dance ahead.
A cup of tea, a twist of fate,
We laugh at how we contemplate.

Through tangled paths in endless jest,
We trip on signs and call it blessed.
Oh joy, to ponder, spin and twirl,
While answers play coy with a whirl.

In every corner, quirks we find,
A riddle wrapped in chaos, blind.
Our minds like jumbled jigsaw pieces,
Creating fun as curiosity increases.

With every turn in our grand escapade,
We shrug at life, a playful charade.
A laugh, a giggle, it takes the cake,
In this odd quest we all partake.

Labyrinth of Thoughts Unraveled

In a maze of ideas, we take a stroll,
With stubbed toes and a comic role.
Each twist and turn, a quirky surprise,
Like socks on a cat, oh how time flies!

Stuck in a junction, do we choose left or right?
It's hard to tell in this funny sight.
With thoughts in a tango, we slip and spin,
Chasing after thoughts to see where we've been.

Along the way, a wise guy grins,
"To find what's lost, unwind your sins."
Barefoot on puzzles, hearts in a quirk,
We revel in this silly artwork.

Another dead-end, what a crazy night!
In search of meaning, we just take flight.
With laughter as our guiding light,
We cheer, embrace the silly fight!

Navigating the Unknown Waters

We sail on ships of giggles grand,
With maps of clouds, not a solid plan.
Our compass spins like a top on spree,
What wonders await? Why, let's just see!

Waves of doubt roll high and low,
We catch a fish, or is it a toe?
With sails of laughter, we float along,
In the sea of life, we sing our song.

A pod of dolphins in tutus dance,
Reminding us of life's silly chance.
With every splash and every surge,
We laugh at how our worries purge.

In navigated chaos, we play the game,
Collecting stories, never the same.
With stars to guide and winks from fate,
We drift away, it's never too late!

The Mystery of Tomorrow's Dawn

As sunrise teases with a wink,
We wonder what tomorrow will think.
Dreaming of pancakes and cats that sing,
In the tribunal of hopes, we find our swing.

What if the sun turns purple today?
Or clouds decide to dance and sway?
With coffee cups raised high above,
We cheer for surprises, laughter, and love.

In shadows of fate, the daylight plays,
A circus of moments in silly displays.
We hop on the train of "maybe or might,"
As echoes of giggles blend with daylight.

Tomorrow's whispers are on the breeze,
With hints of madness and shapes that tease.
So let's embrace what's yet to be,
In this grand jest, we laugh full and free!

Waiting for Enlightenment

I sat on a rock, with my snack in hand,
Waiting for wisdom to make its grand stand.
The birds were just chirping, their own little tune,
While I pondered the secrets of stars and the moon.

The rumors were swirling, like clouds up above,
They said if I waited, I'd learn how to love.
But all I got was a sunburn and ants,
And the deep, profound question: Do squirrels wear pants?

I asked an old turtle, so wise and so slow,
He chuckled and said, "Just enjoy the show!"
With snacks and some giggles, I'll take my sweet time,
Who needs all the answers? I've got the best rhyme!

So here I shall linger, with laughter and cheer,
For wisdom's a journey, not a race, I hear.
I'll laugh 'til I cry, and enjoy what I find,
For the search is the fun, and the fun is divine!

Signs Yet to be Seen

I searched for some signs, on a post-it or board,
A cosmic message, or some witty word.
Instead, I found coffee, some crumbs, and the cat,
Who stared at me blankly, like, "What's up with that?"

I looked at the stars, trying hard to discern,
If they could give hints, or just watch and learn.
They twinkled and winked, all up in the night,
But none had a clue, just a cosmic delight.

Oh, I thought I saw thunder, a flash of the wise,
But it turned out to be just a couple of flies!
They buzzed 'round my head, all confused by the light,
And here I was waiting for answers all night.

So, I'll heed what they say, with a chuckle and grin,
Sometimes the best signs are the giggles within.
Let the universe jest; it's a comedian's scene,
There's laughter aplenty in all that's unseen!

The Great Unknown

In the depths of my thoughts, there's a vast, open space,
Filled with wild questions, each wearing a face.
I wrote them all down in a notebook so neat,
But somehow, they danced, and just ran on their feet.

One question was dressed in a polka-dot suit,
It giggled and bounced, oh so silly and cute.
Another wore glasses, each lens a black hole,
As they pondered life's meaning, or at least their next role.

They started a party, right there in my mind,
With cake and confetti, and fun of all kinds.
I joined in the chaos, and leaped with delight,
For who needs all the answers when laughter takes flight?

So cheers to the unknown, my friends, take a seat!
With a curious heart, and a rhythm so sweet.
Life's a magical journey, with quirks to explore,
Let's dance in the questions and crave even more!

Conversations with Silence

I sat down with silence, just sipping my tea,
"Tell me your secrets," I said with glee.
But silence just chuckled and stared back at me,
Like, "What's so profound? Can't you just let it be?"

I tried asking questions, profound and sincere,
But silence just waved, "I can't really hear!"
I brought in a drummer, a kazoo and a flute,
To coax out the wisdom, oh, what a hoot!

In the void, there's a giggle, a snicker or two,
It seems even silence loves a good view.
With rhythms and jokes, it twirled round my head,
As we laughed at the ponderings left unsaid.

So here's to our chats with the calm and the still,
Where laughter erupts, and time bends to thrill.
For in every "why" whispered, in every small pause,
Are the treasures of joy, and perhaps even flaws!

Whispered Hopes in the Abyss

In a chasm deep and wide,
Hope's whispers dare to hide.
Were they lost or just on break?
Perhaps they're out for cake!

Echoes bounce from wall to wall,
"Did we mean to take this fall?"
With laughter ringing, joy ensues,
Maybe they just changed their views!

Adventures of the Awoken Mind

My brain awoke with a thud,
Ready to conquer all the mud.
"Hey, let's ponder every plight!"
But then I just took a bite!

Thoughts raced fast but lost their track,
One led me to a rabbit snack.
Search for answers, but oh surprise,
Found a donut, what a prize!

Eternal Questions

Why's the sky, oh, blue and bright?
Is there cheese in every bite?
Questions swirl like autumn leaves,
Yet my mind just tricks and weaves.

Do ducks ever think of flight?
And who invented day and night?
With giggles mixed in every quest,
Life's full of curious jest!

Awaiting Epiphanies

Waiting here with bated breath,
For brilliance that escapes certain death.
Did I heed the signs last night?
Or did that chocolate cake take flight?

Mind's a web of tangled threads,
Full of chocolates, dreams, and breads.
With a grin, I sit and ponder,
Maybe I just need to wander!

Dances with Destiny

In the ballroom of fate we twirl,
Frilly questions make our minds whirl.
With every step, we're lost in a sea,
Who knew existence could be so free?

Spinning wildly, we bump into chance,
Tripping over dreams in this cosmic dance.
Feet tangled up, we laugh and play,
Wondering what the stars will say.

A waltz with worries, a jig with fate,
Each misstep feels like a first date.
With every stumble, we giggle and sigh,
Who needs a plan when you can fly?

So let's dance on this puzzling floor,
With life's questions begging for more.
Just don't step on my toes, my friend,
The clock is ticking, but it's not the end.

Moments of Hesitation

Standing at life's crossroads, oh so unsure,
With choices like candy, how can we be pure?
Do we pick door number one, two, or three?
Is it a game show, or just life's cup of tea?

A glance at the future reveals silly sights,
Unicorns dancing in pajamas at night.
What's the hold-up? Why do we pause?
Is it fear, or just a break for applause?

Every step feels like we're on a stage,
Playing a part on life's whimsical page.
Shall we leap forward or take a small bow?
Oh, moments of hesitation, why do you plague us now?

But maybe the fun is in sitting still,
Waiting for answers that never fulfill.
So let's stretch and yawn in this funny old game,
Tomorrow's a mystery, but today's quite the same.

The Puzzle of Existence

Life's a puzzle with missing pieces,
One day it fits, then chaos increases.
Where's the corner? And where's the edge?
Part art, part science, part playful hedge.

We search for the blue sky in a box of gray,
Counting the reasons, come what may.
Oh, if I had a quarter for every clue,
I'd buy a ticket to an existential zoo!

With cats wearing hats and dogs that dream,
Life's colorful circus can make us scream.
Is that the answer or just a hoot?
Oh, puzzles are funny when they don't compute.

So let's chuckle at the mess of our fate,
Throw in our pieces, "What's the wait?"
For in this confusion, we often find glee,
The puzzle, though missing, is still a spree.

The Gaps Between Answers

Between the questions, there's space and cheer,
Like awkward silences, we hold them dear.
A chuckle here, a scratch of the head,
Are those crickets I hear or thoughts being fed?

The gaps in our knowledge, a comical sight,
Like socks without partners, they dance in the night.
Missing pieces causing laughter to flow,
Why do we panic? Just let it go slow!

In every pause, joy may just burst,
As we ponder and fumble with our crazy thirst.
What's 'out there'? Who knows, let's just assume,
That the universe loves to jest and to bloom.

So, here's to the in-betweens, the funny delay,
The giggles we share as we wander astray.
Let's embrace the gaps, may they linger and sway,
For life's best jokes are just questions at play.

Quandaries in the Quiet

In the silence, thoughts collide,
Questions swirling, nowhere to hide.
Coffee cups filled with doubts run deep,
Lost in the maze, I try not to weep.

Why do socks vanish in the wash?
Is the universe just one big nosh?
The cat stares at me, plotting my fate,
While I ponder on why I'm always late.

The ceiling fan hums a tune so sweet,
It asks if I've chosen the right seat.
Are we but players in a cosmic jest?
Or just confused sprouts on life's great quest?

I crack a joke about time's sly trick,
As seconds slip by, thick as a brick.
The clock laughs, its hands spin around,
Making hours seem like lost and found.

Mysteries of the Mind

My brain's a puzzle, pieces amiss,
Like a jigsaw that misses a fist.
Thoughts flash like lightning, then fade away,
What did I come in here to say?

The fridge hums secrets I never asked,
While I ponder a question so masked.
Are bread crumbs the universe's delight?
Or just snacks for a long, lonely night?

I sit in circles, repeating my fate,
Chasing answers I can't navigate.
The goldfish watches with bulging eyes,
As I yearn for wisdom, but find only fries.

With humor like a scarf, wrapped so tight,
I laugh at why we all take flight.
Are we simply birds in a cosmic dance?
Or just fools hoping for a second chance?

The Canvas of Confusion

Colors clash on my brain's canvas wide,
What's wrong with this picture, I can't decide.
Is clarity hiding behind a door?
Or did it sneak out for a quick tour?

I doodle questions in the margins low,
Like why does the toaster never know?
Is the bread too smart, or am I too dull?
A riddle in the morning, it's quite a pull!

Creativity spills like paint from a can,
Each splatter's a part of my master plan.
But as I paint dreams in abstract strokes,
The canvas just laughs, surrounded by jokes.

So I brush with laughter, not fear or pain,
As I muse on the links of this wild chain.
Are we the artists of our own fate?
Or just clowns waiting at life's first gate?

Perpetual Paradoxes

Do I run from wisdom, or chase it down?
Why does the lost always wear a crown?
The chicken crossed the road, but why?
To find a question with wings to fly!

Mirrors reflect who we think we are,
Yet the truth hides somewhere near a star.
I ponder deep as I sit on the grass,
Counting my blessings that come to pass.

The world spins tales like a child with clay,
Sculpting odd shapes in a delightful way.
Is the meaning lost on the fun of the ride?
Or found in the laughter we can't ever hide?

So here's to the whims of paradox grand,
Where logic and humor go hand in hand.
In the end, are we just a joke told in jest?
Or a cosmic pun in the universe's chest?

Unraveled Mysteries

Clocks tick slowly in my mind,
While questions dance, forever entwined.
I seek the secrets held so tight,
In the quirky corners of my night.

Puppies ponder profound debates,
Bacon dreams, and lots of plates.
With every riddle comes a giggle,
Is that laughter or a wiggle?

The cat has wisdom, or so I've heard,
As it plots world domination with just one word.
I question fate while eating pie,
As stars above shout, "Oh my, oh my!"

So here I stand, a puzzled fool,
Searching signs inside a swimming pool.
Answers in bubbles, fleeting and bright,
But the joy's in the quest, and oh what a sight!

Specters of Possibility

Ghosts of questions float in air,
Haunting dreams without a care.
They nibble at my thoughts each day,
While socks mysteriously drift away.

What does it mean when toast goes burnt?
Is that a sign, or just my hurt?
Spelling bees in my cereal bowl,
Piece by piece, they take their toll.

I ask the sun, I ask the moon,
"Why can't I sing a happy tune?"
They chuckle back, in cosmic glee,
As I trip over my own two feet.

So I'll dance with shadows, waltz in jest,
And laugh aloud, it's all for the best.
With every mishap, I'll wear a grin,
For life's a show, let the silliness win!

Chasing the Elusive

I chase a thought, it runs away,
Playing tag in a bright display.
Like soap bubbles that float and gleam,
Life's riddles feel like a wild dream.

The unicorns plot while I just stall,
In a land where nothing seems too small.
I juggle clowns and giggle wide,
As the mysteries take me for a ride.

Hats fly off, and shoes go astray,
In this circus of whimsy, I must say.
Yet amidst the chaos, laughter reigns,
Each jolt and joy spills in bright trains.

So if you ask about the great unknown,
Just follow the socks that have brightly flown.
For within the dance, the humor unfolds,
And the truth might just be that laughter is gold.

Beneath the Surface

Under the waves, a fish wears a hat,
With googly eyes, it's quite a chat!
"What's life like?" I ask with glee,
"It's just me and the thoughts of tea!"

The octopus shrugs, all eight arms flail,
"I lost my pen, but can still tell a tale!"
Bubbles of questions rise to the skies,
As the jellyfish float with curious sighs.

I dive deeper, looking for clues,
Amongst the corals, yellow and blues.
The rocks just giggle, "You seek too much,
Just dance with the waves, that's our touch!"

So here's to the depths, both funny and bright,
Where laughter bubbles in the silvery light.
Seeking answers beneath all the fun,
Life's a quirky race, and we've just begun!

A Tapestry of Unanswered Dreams

In the loom of thoughts we weave,
A tapestry of dreams we leave.
Spinning tales with silly threads,
Chasing answers in our heads.

Joke on a shelf, it gathers dust,
While we all ponder what we must.
Is it frogs or maybe cheese?
Oh, life, you're such a tease!

We seek wisdom through this dance,
But only find a jester's chance.
Every riddle throws a curve,
Yet we giggle and preserve.

So, grab your hat, let's take a ride,
In the circus where truths collide.
We'll laugh until the stars align,
And toast to life's grand punchline!

Threads of Existence Tangled

Life's a ball of tangled yarn,
Knots and loops can cause alarm.
We pull and tug, hoping for sense,
But instead find wacky recompense.

Questions bounce like rubber balls,
While logic dances down the halls.
Should I ask the cheese or cat?
Are they wise? Or just plain fat?

Philosophers with frosty brews,
Musing life with comic views.
Yearning for a cosmic cheat,
They doodle answers on the seat.

Perhaps it's best to just enjoy,
The playful chaos life can toy.
For in this mess, we find our glee,
In tangled threads, we're wild and free!

The Pursuit of Perpetual Questions

Why do ducks quack in a row?
Where does the wind go when it blows?
The universe giggles in disguise,
While we seek truths with curious eyes.

Why do socks disappear in wash?
Is there a cosmic socky posh?
We ponder, laugh, and scratch our heads,
While chasing mysteries like silly threads.

Queries pile like laundry's peak,
We search for answers, yet stay weak.
Does the cat know where they hide?
Does it laugh while we confide?

So let's embrace this riddle spree,
With laughter ringing like a key.
In every question, joy we'll find,
As life teases our curious mind!

Footprints on a Path Unseen

Upon this path, there's a dance,
With footprints that lead to happenstance.
Each step we take is filled with jest,
Wondering what we've yet to quest.

Do fish really swim with a plan?
Or is there more to their fishy clan?
As we stumble on, we laugh and play,
On this puzzling, wobbly pathway.

Confused yet curious, we wander wide,
Finding joy in the doubts we bide.
Every pathway says, 'come explore!'
And life just giggles, asking for more!

Let's skip along to the unknown,
With unanswered questions, we have grown.
Embracing quirks in every twist,
In this whimsical chase, we persist!

The Odyssey of Understanding

In a ship of thought, we sail so far,
Navigating through the cosmic bazaar.
Questions like jellyfish float in the sea,
Their stings are puzzling, oh woe is me!

With charts that are scribbles and maps that are jokes,
We're captured by riddles and riddle-smoke.
Each star a dilemma, each wave a quirk,
Trying to decipher, we're still at work!

The compass spins wildly, it just can't decide,
If 'left' is the answer or 'right' is the ride.
Oh, the irony thickens like cream in the tea,
As we dine on confusion, just you wait and see!

But laughter abounds in this voyage so grand,
For every wild question deserves a helping hand.
So we dance with the mysteries, chuckling along,
In this absurd odyssey, where we all belong.

Enigmas of Emotion

A feeling pops up, like toast from a pan,
Sweet as a cookie, or bitter, oh man!
One moment I'm joyful, the next in despair,
Emotions are marbles that roll everywhere!

With faces that squinch like a squirrel in flight,
We juggle our feelings from morning to night.
Laughter like confetti, cries like a rain,
Processing the chaos can drive one insane!

A puzzle of giggles wrapped in a sigh,
Like trying to catch a cloud passing by.
One second I'm dancing, the next I'm a statue,
Emotion's a circus, and I'm the main act too!

Yet in this grand mess, we smile with ease,
For each complex feeling is a slice of cheese.
So let's feast on the flavors, both rich and absurd,
In this banquet of feelings, every dish is heard.

The Faint Glimmer

A light at the end, or just a trick of the eye?
We stumble and fumble, oh my, oh my!
This glimmer of wisdom, so faint and so small,
Like a firefly's dance at a summer night's ball.

We chase it in circles, around and around,
Like a cat chasing shadows on sunlit ground.
Is it real or a mirage, this flicker we seek?
Our brains are like sponges, yet still feel so weak!

What does it mean? Can it really be true?
Could it solve all the puzzles that baffle me and you?
With questions that spiral like spaghetti on plates,
The light pulls us closer as we contemplate fates!

But in this pursuit, let's enjoy every jest,
For the journey is lite, and the laughter's the best.
So let's lean in together, with curiosity,
This faint glimmer leads us to camaraderie!

Underneath the Questions

Beneath all the wonder, lies a great pile of 'why',
Like a Pokemon hiding, but oh, so sly.
Each inquiry bubbles, like soda in pop,
As we dive into chaos, we'll never just stop!

With why's flapping wings like a butterfly's dream,
Fluttering 'round, causing a cognitive scream.
Questions do pirouettes, then land with a thud,
Messy as frosting, or a mud pie of fun!

What if we're stardust, or just a neat trick?
With answers a puzzle, we play with a flick.
Each question a party, we bring the confetti,
Let's dance through the queries, the mood is all heady!

So grab a curiosity, let's see what it holds,
Underneath the questions, a treasure unfolds.
We laugh at the riddles, share a giggle or two,
For the joy's in the journey, and the fun's here for you!

Echoes of Uncertainty

In a room full of questions, we wonder aloud,
Are we right, are we wrong? It's all a bit loud.
The answers keep dancing, just out of reach,
Like a cat with a laser, they giggle and screech.

So we gather together, a curious bunch,
Playing puzzles of life over pancakes for lunch.
With forks and with dreams strewn across the floor,
We eat up our doubts like a fine gourmet store.

With each clink of glasses, we toast and we cheer,
To mysteries lingering and laughter we hear.
Oh, the joy of the questions that dance in the night,
As we giggle and ponder, our future feels bright.

So here's to the inquiries, big and small,
To the quests we embark on, and the brainiacs' call.
Life's quirks are the spice to our curiosity stew,
And the flavor we're mixing could still use a clue.

Whispers of Tomorrow

Tomorrow's a whisper, a cheeky little sprite,
With secrets tucked under her blanket of light.
She winks at the sunrise, a promise unmade,
As we juggle our wishes, trying not to evade.

We tiptoe through futures, a dance full of flair,
With dreams like balloons, floating high in the air.
But then come the seagulls, they squawk and they caw,
Stealing ideas like a ravenous maw.

Plans scribbled on napkins, so fragile, so bright,
One gust of confusion can take them from sight.
So we laugh at the chaos, the tumble, the spin,
Because while we're all lost, you've gotta dive in.

With giggles and gigabytes, we navigate trends,
Writing tomorrows like letters to friends.
Who knows what will come next, it's a thrill and a jest,
In the end, we just hope for a nap and some rest.

Shadows of Inquiry

In shadows of questions, we wander and roam,
Chasing flickers of answers that feel far from home.
Like detectives with capes, we scribble our clues,
Playing hide-and-seek with our own made-up news.

The walls echo laughter, absurd and off-key,
As we ponder if fish ever dream of the sea.
We question the universe, with snacks in our hands,
Trying to catch thoughts like they're grains of fine sand.

With each riddle we tackle, our faces turn bright,
Like kids on a treasure hunt, hearts filled with delight.
So here's to the puzzles that twinkle and tease,
May our funny inquiries bring us to our knees.

Let's toast to the queries, the silly and grand,
To the mixed-up perspectives that life has planned.
For within every question, a chuckle is found,
And a sprinkle of wonder that knows no bound.

Clocks That Don't Tock

Tick-tock goes the clock, or does it just sigh?
Time's like a magician, it waves and says bye.
With clocks that don't tock, we lounge and we play,
In a world where forever feels like a buffet.

Life's seconds are donuts, each sweet bite we take,
Do we nibble on minutes or gobble the cake?
With whims of our heartbeat, we dance 'neath the stars,
While pondering if time is just hiding in jars.

So gather your spoons and don't worry at all,
For the silence of seconds we'll gladly enthrall.
With laughter and warmth as our compass and guide,
We'll savor the moments that ebb and reside.

So whether the clock is just taking a break,
Or sailing on waves that it just couldn't shake,
We'll find joy in the breezes, the pauses, the jest,
Knowing life's quirky rhythm is truly the best.

Navigating Ambiguity

In a world of questions, it's tough to find,
The maps are all blurry, I'm lost in my mind.
I search for the signs, a guide that can speak,
But laughter erupts, as clarity's weak.

With riddles and puzzles, I wade through the mess,
A jester of reason, can you really guess?
Is it green light or red? I just can't decide,
Oh look, a goat! Just let confusion slide.

The experts are here, with charts and with graphs,
But their serious faces just make me laugh.
In quantum quandaries, I twirl and I spin,
Maybe I'll find it, or just go for ice cream.

So here in the fog, I embrace the unknown,
With humor my beacon, I stroll all alone.
If wisdom is waiting, it's hiding quite sly,
I'll sip on absurdity, and wave good-bye.

Roads Less Traveled

I take the wrong turn on this winding road,
The signs are confusing, like noodles unbowed.
I ask for directions, get lost in a tale,
Of sharks in the trees and a cat with a pail.

There's laughter in stumbles, in every wrong track,
With detours that sparkle, no need to look back.
I meet quirky strangers, who share quirky dreams,
While riding on scooters with wheels like moonbeams.

Each bend that I take leads to comedy gold,
With stories of misfits, so thrillingly bold.
While searching for answers, I slip on a charm,
Life's pinball machine keeps me safe from all harm.

So here's to the roads that don't follow the plan,
With bumpy adventures, I shine like a fan.
If wisdom's a journey, I'll dance through the blips,
With laughter the fuel for my whimsical trips.

Whirlwinds of Reflection

In a tempest of thoughts, I whirl and I spin,
Chasing after ideas that always begin.
A riddle of mirrors reflects with great zeal,
While I ponder the essence of every meal.

I talk to my thoughts, they giggle and tease,
As shadows of notions dance in the breeze.
A cat with a monocle ponders the deep,
While I trip over questions I thought I could keep.

With spirals of humor and blunders galore,
I search for the meaning while slipping on lore.
Each whirl of confusion means laughter is near,
In the chaos of thoughts, clarity's cheer.

So let's twirl in the chaos, embrace what we find,
The whirlwinds of thinking, so comical and kind.
If the meaning is hidden, I'll laugh with a grin,
For the journey of searching is where we begin.

Crescendo of Questions

In a symphony grand, the questions arise,
With trumpets of wonder, and curious sighs.
I ask if the moon is made out of cheese,
The answers get funnier with each tiny tease.

With percussion of ponder, the drums beat away,
Each query a note in a wild cabaret.
Do ducks wear pajamas? Is time really bent?
These musings keep spinning, no need to lament.

A crescendo of chaos, a chorus of fun,
As I juggle my thoughts, they skip one by one.
With violins whining about life's grand quest,
What is the point? Who needs to invest?

So here's to the laughter amidst all the fuss,
A crescendo of questions, together we discuss.
If answers are hidden, let's giggle and sway,
For joy in the asking is always okay.

In Search of an Illusive Horizon

Chasing sunsets on a Tuesday,
I trip on dreams, not quite ballet.
With every step, I glance behind,
Where answers play a game, unkind.

A squirrel mocks my serious fall,
While clouds just smile, no care at all.
"Try harder!" echoes in my mind,
But clarity's a trick, so blind.

I wonder if they stay at bay,
These truths that hide, like kids at play.
I'll barbecue instead, sounds fun,
And let the questions melt in sun.

They say the journey's what we seek,
Yet here I am, just feeling weak.
Maybe a snack will set things right,
And bring forth wisdom, just tonight.

Echoes of What Is Not Yet

In the hallway of my thoughts,
I hear echoes of tangled knots.
Whispers say, "It's coming soon,"
But I tripped over a silly tune.

A cat looks up, and I just sigh,
Wondering if I should just fly.
The clock ticks loud, but does it care?
Time's just teasing with a dare.

I juggle lemons, throw them high,
Might as well see if they can fly.
A grin appears, my face a mess,
Perhaps confusion's just success?

So here I dance, a touch absurd,
Chasing all those half-heard words.
With every laugh, I feel alive,
In this waiting game, I will thrive.

Unraveled Threads of Being

I knit a scarf with thoughts so loose,
A fashion sense that's quite obtuse.
Each stitch a question, wildly thrown,
With every loop, my mind has grown.

A sock appears, but oh, what's that?
It's lost a mate; it's now a brat.
Did I just wander off the path?
Or is this comedy, pure math?

The universe laughs at my plight,
As I unravel fears at night.
A cup of tea, warm, helps me chill,
While pondering if I need more skill.

I gather threads from all around,
In this rush, I seek a sound.
Perhaps a song will close the gap,
While I remember where I wrapped.

The Space Between Certainty and Doubt

I sit between a rock and roll,
Two options dance, they take a toll.
Should I eat cake or take a jog?
Both paths are clear; I still feel fog.

The scales are tipping in my head,
Counting calories, then I'm led.
To sketch a map for senseless bliss,
But doubt throws pies; oh, what a twist!

A chicken's crossing, or so they say,
With crossed-out plans that fade away.
As irony walks in the door,
I ponder if I've lost the score.

Yet here I laugh, a light brigade,
In this vast realm where doubts invade.
With every giggle, I reclaim,
The joy of just forgetting names.

Answers That Never Arrive

I asked the stars up in the sky,
They chuckled back, they don't reply.
A fortune cookie gave a grin,
But all it said was 'Try again.'

I wrote a letter to the moon,
She spun around, said 'Not so soon!'
The universe just loves to tease,
While I keep searching for some keys.

My coffee cup spilled out a clue,
Suggesting that I take a brew.
But all it did was burn my hand,
And left me with no grand plan.

I turned to Google, bold and bright,
It told me 'This is not your night.'
The answers hide, just out of reach,
While life's a wacky, messy beach.

Unfinished Thoughts

I pondered deep, as shadows yawn,
And then forgot what I was on.
My brain's a maze, a tangled web,
Of half-formed dreams I try to ebb.

A squirrel chattered, loud and clear,
I thought it knew the truth I fear.
But all it did was chase a nut,
Leaving me in quite the rut.

I jotted down a spark of light,
Then spilled my drink; it was a sight!
The ink ran wild, began to swim,
My grand ideas now look quite dim.

So here I sit, with pen and sigh,
These unfinished thoughts just wave goodbye.
But what if chaos is the key?
Perhaps the nonsense sets me free!

The Quest for Meaning

I set off on a grand crusade,
With snacks and drinks and plans well laid.
But every trail led to a mall,
Where I just wandered, lost, and small.

I chased a rabbit, swift and spry,
It turned around and made me cry.
It winked and vanished in thin air,
Leaving me with naught but hair.

The compass spun like a dancer,
I thought to drink from fate's small canister.
Instead, it spilled on my new shoes,
Now I'm a mess with these old blues.

But still I grin and carry forth,
For purpose lies in quirky worth.
Perhaps I'll find a hidden sign,
On what to eat for lunch, divine!

In Pursuit of Clarity

I wear my glasses, scratch my head,
And question things I thought I said.
A signpost danced with neon lights,
But all it said was 'Take your sights.'

I asked my cat, she licked her paw,
Suggesting I might rethink law.
But fluff and fur don't hold the truth,
Only crumbs and lost time's sleuth.

The clouds above seemed oddly shaped,
Perhaps they're just the dreams I draped.
Yet whispers swirl in silly jest,
As I keep seeking, humor's best.

So on I trot, with grin and glee,
In this wild ride, just let it be.
Maybe space is where we spark,
And find our way in the absurd dark.

 www.ingramcontent.com/pod-product-compliance
Lightning Source LLC
Chambersburg PA
CBHW071851160426
43209CB00003B/513